KINDNESS ROCKS JOURNAL

Turner Publishing Company

Nashville, Tennessee

www.turnerpublishing.com

Layout & Cover Design: Elina Diaz

Library of Congress Cataloging-in-Publication number: 2019938544 ISBN: (print) 978-1-64250-082-0, (ebook) 978-1-64250-083-7 BISAC category code: SELF-HELP / A irmations

Printed in the United States of America

KINDNESS ROCKS JOURNAL

An Interactive Space to Work Through
Difficult Times and Create Inspiring
Messages to Share with Others

MEGAN MURPHY

Founder of The Kindness Rocks Project

TURNER
PUBLISHING COMPANY

Introduction

Thank you for your purchase of *The Kindness Rocks Journal*. This is the first step toward making yourself a priority and taking some much needed time for personal reflection.

The following rock prompts aim to heighten personal insight and generate a greater perspective that will benefit not only yourself, but those around you as well.

Each inspirational message presented by way of a Kindness Rock may have many meanings depending on what situations you are currently dealing with. That is why we have created this reflective journal. One rock message can have a completely different meaning for various life situations and/or experiences. No two people will view a rock in the same way. Our past experiences and perceptions generate our reaction to the prompts.

Becoming curious and reflective is the first step toward living a more authentic and joyful life. Today, many of us are distracted by social media, hectic life/work schedules, and unrealistic expectations that we assign to ourselves, so we rarely take time to reflect. To be honest, often reflection can bring up thoughts that we would rather not give our attention to. It is important to be able to "allow" these thoughts to come and go, through curiosity. Our thoughts often appear as "white noise," meaning they arise as subliminal negative self-talk which we rarely question. We simply accept this noise rather than questioning where it stems from.

We all have this negative self-talk, and the keys to overcoming it are quiet and reflection. I realize this sounds counterproductive as, in the silence, you might expect the noise to get louder. It is just the opposite. Trust the process. When we sit and focus our attention on these thoughts and challenge them, they seem to evaporate. The quiet actually drowns out the noise and, lo and behold, a different voice arises. This voice is nourishing, self-assured, and truthful. This is the voice that has been trying to get your attention, and, in the quiet, she will reveal herself and come out of hiding. She has been waiting for you to notice her and, once you do, she will help guide the way toward living your beautiful, authentic life.

When we take the time to reflect upon the things that bring us joy and we are grateful for, we become more aware of these things as they show up in our everyday lives. We then begin to look for the "good" in each moment rather than focusing our attention on the negative things happening in the world around us. We become a light for others by cultivating a greater, kinder, and more compassionate perspective.

May these prompts provide you with the insight you are seeking, and may you then begin to share this greater wisdom with others; each one of us has a responsibility to leave this world a better place than we found it!

In Gratitude,
Megan Murphy
Founder of The Kindness Rocks Project

How to Use This Journal

This journal was created for all of the kind souls who have followed and joined The Kindness Rocks Project because you felt a tug at your heart to do so. Thank you for spreading kindness in your community. It is important to take time to return that kindness to yourself!

Your interest in this journal is an indication that you are curious about finding more joy in your life. The Kindness Rocks Project community is ready to embrace you and help guide you through this self-reflective experience. There is a rather large group of project members across the globe here to support and encourage you along the way as you discover the powerful combination of self-reflection and kindness and the impact it can have on your life.

Keep your journal handy, on your nightstand or by your favorite chair, so that you will be reminded to take time daily for reflection. Let this journal act as a reflective guide rather than as yet another thing to do on that never-ending to-do list of yours. Writing in this journal daily is a simple way to find peace among all of the chaos— one day, one page at a time.

All around the world, there are many, just like you, embarking on a journey of self-reflection and self-discovery. Join us on social media by using the hashtag #TheKindnessRocksProject. There you will discover many more reflective Kindness Rock messages created by other creative project members. There is so much we can learn about ourselves and even more to discover about others when we look for ways to connect with one another. We are all the same kind of different, and when we heighten our compassion and empathy for others, we increase it for ourselves.

WE
NEED TO TREAT
OTHERS
PEOPLE
THE WAY THEY
WANT
TO BE TREATED

drop the Rock

"WE NEED TO TREAT OTHERS THE WAY WE WANT TO BE TREATED."
—THE GOLDEN RULE

Reflect on a time when someone unexpectedly offered you a compliment or did a kind gesture for you. How did that make you feel? You may wish to include thoughts about your initial reaction as well as the lasting impression it made on you.

_____

_____

_____

_____

_____

_____

_____

_____

_____

_____

_____

_____

_____

_____

_____

_____

_____

_____

_____

_____

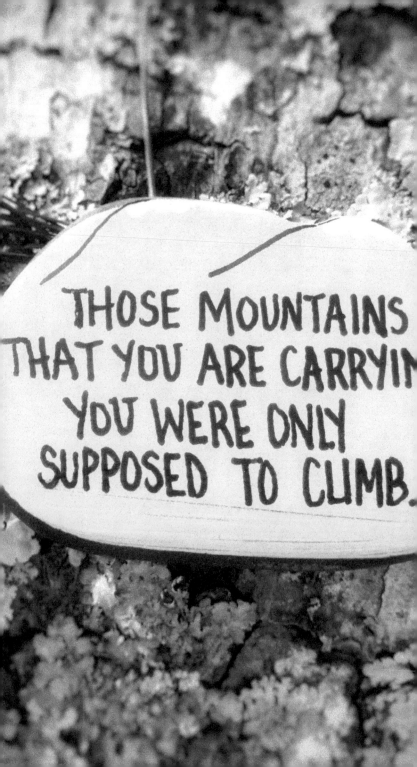

> "THESE MOUNTAINS THAT YOU ARE CARRYING,
> YOU WERE ONLY SUPPOSED TO CLIMB."
> —NAJWA ZEBIAN

We all feel overwhelmed from time to time. Reflect upon a time when you felt overwhelmed and how you overcame that feeling. What steps did you take? How did you feel when that moment passed?

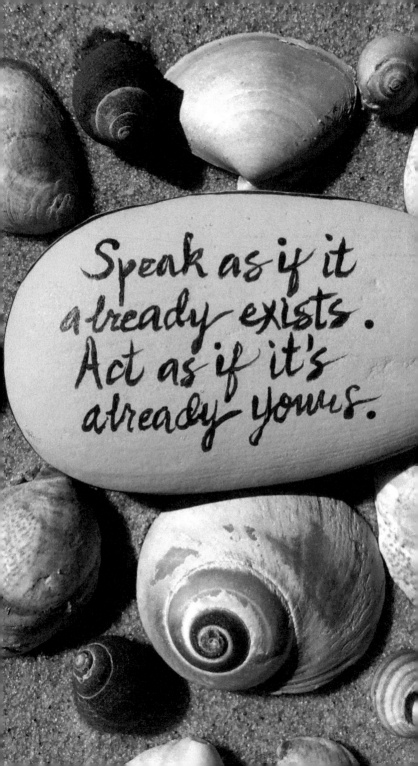

"SPEAK AS IF IT ALREADY EXISTS. ACT AS IF IT'S ALREADY YOURS."
—LAW OF ATTRACTION

When we give voice to our dreams and intentions, we call them into our awareness. We amplify the intentions through our words and thoughts. Write about a goal you wish to achieve in the past tense, as if you have already achieved it. Visualize and add details.

Change my friends... is ON US!

CHANGE, MY FRIENDS, IS ON US!

The unknown tends to conjure up fear and prevent us from making a change. Reflect on a time when you were afraid to try something new. How did it feel when you pushed back the fear and accomplished it?

_____

_____

_____

_____

_____

_____

_____

_____

_____

_____

_____

_____

_____

_____

_____

_____

_____

_____

_____

_____

I BELIEVE IN ME.

The first person you must convince is you. You must believe in yourself and then take steps toward whatever it is that brings you joy! What are three traits you posess that you are proud of?

_____

_____

_____

_____

_____

_____

_____

_____

_____

_____

_____

_____

_____

_____

_____

_____

_____

_____

_____

_____

_____

_____

YOU CAN!

List three things you have done that you didn't think you could do. Next, list three things that you hope to do in the future.

HERE IT COMES, ANOTHER BLESSING!

Always be on the lookout for blessings. Often, they arise
unexpectedly and in disguise. Reflect on the many blessings in your
life. How did they arrive? Write about your many blessings or simply
reflect on your biggest blessing yet.

"You are free to make your own choices, but you will never be free of the consequences of your choices."

–Srishti

"WRINKLES ONLY GO WHERE THE SMILES HAVE BEEN."

—JIMMY BUFFETT, LYRICS TO "BAREFOOT CHILDREN"

Write about something or someone who makes you smile.

I hear & I forget. I see & I Remember. I do & I Understand!

~ Confucius

> "I HEAR AND I FORGET. I SEE AND I REMEMBER.
> I DO AND I UNDERSTAND."
>
> —CONFUCIUS

We all need to be reminded now and again about what matters most. Engaging in volunteer activities or showing kindness toward others lifts our mood and makes us feel better. Today, go out in your community and then use this page to reflect upon the kind act you completed and how it made you feel.

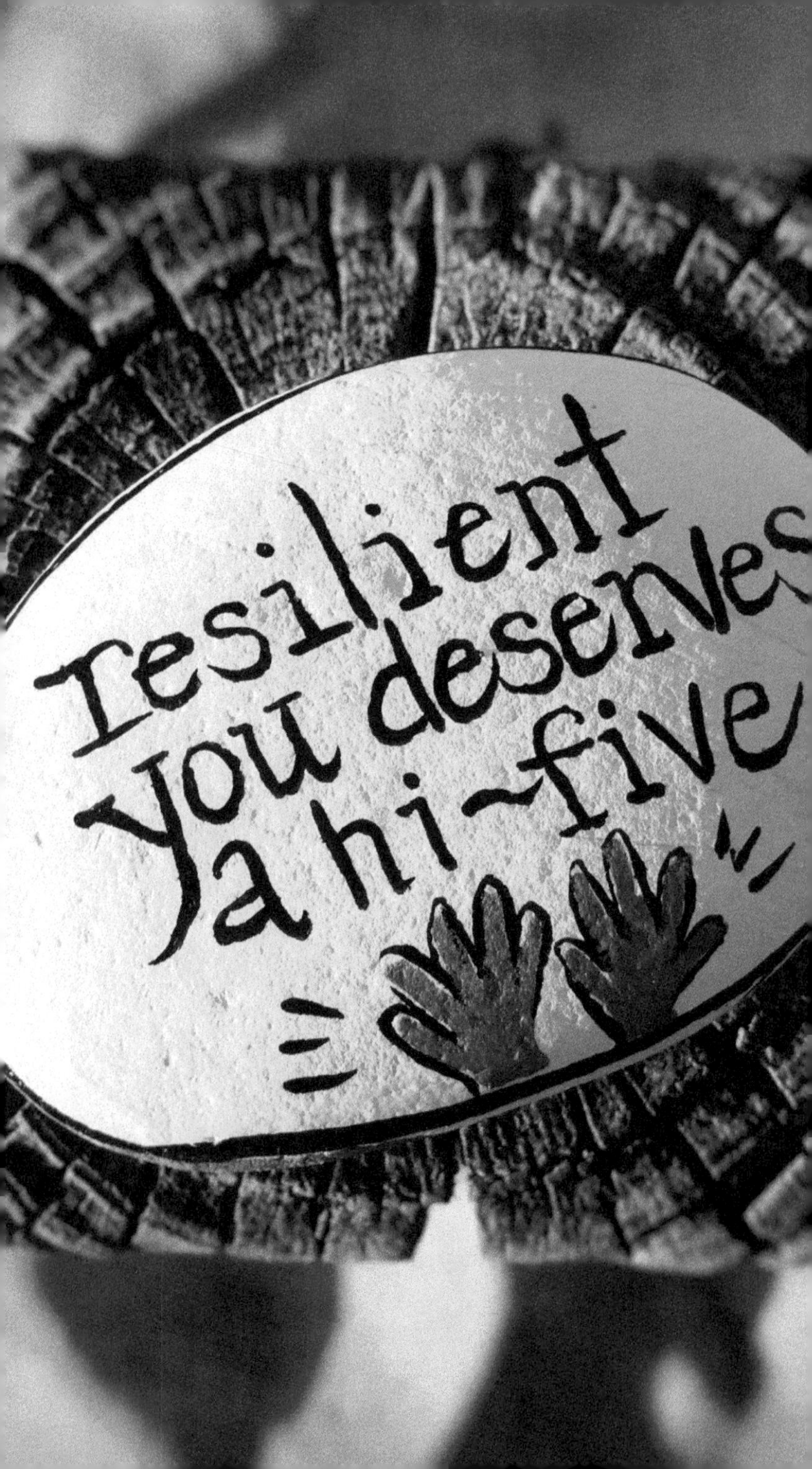
resilient
You deserves
a hi~five

RESILIENT YOU DESERVES A HIGH-FIVE.

When was the last time you gave yourself a high-five?
List three things that you have done that deserve a high-five.

One day we will all come to realize that the small simple moments were really the big moments after all.

"ONE DAY WE WILL ALL COME TO REALIZE THAT THE SMALL,
SIMPLE MOMENTS WERE REALLY THE BIG MOMENTS AFTER ALL."

—MEGAN MURPHY

At the end of the day, what were the small, everyday moments that
had the greatest impact on you?

_____

_____

_____

_____

_____

_____

_____

_____

_____

_____

_____

_____

_____

_____

_____

_____

_____

_____

_____

_____

You can't
Cross the Sea merely
By standing and Starin
at the Water

"YOU CAN'T CROSS THE SEA MERELY BY STANDING

AND STARING AT THE WATER."

—RABINDRANATH TAGORE

Who or what motivates you?

_____

_____

_____

_____

_____

_____

_____

_____

_____

_____

_____

_____

_____

_____

_____

_____

_____

_____

_____

_____

_____

Everybody has a story. And there is something to be learned from every experience. ~Oprah

"EVERYBODY HAS A STORY. AND THERE IS SOMETHING TO BE LEARNED

FROM EVERY EXPERIENCE."

—OPRAH WINFREY

Reflect on an experience you had that was difficult and the valuable life lesson learned from it.

I'm actually
deeply grateful that
some things didn't wo
out the way I
wanted them t

I'M ACTUALLY DEEPLY GRATEFUL THAT SOME THINGS DIDN'T WORK OUT THE WAY I WANTED THEM TO.

Imagine if everything you wished for came true. So often, we are unaware that our wishes may actually interfere with a bigger plan or picture for our lives. For example, that relationship that didn't work out. You were left heartbroken and yet, many years later, you met the love of your life. Interesting how that happens. Reflect on one of these situations in your life and begin writing by using the phrase "I trust that..."

_____

_____

_____

_____

_____

_____

_____

_____

_____

_____

_____

_____

_____

_____

_____

_____

_____

_____

_____

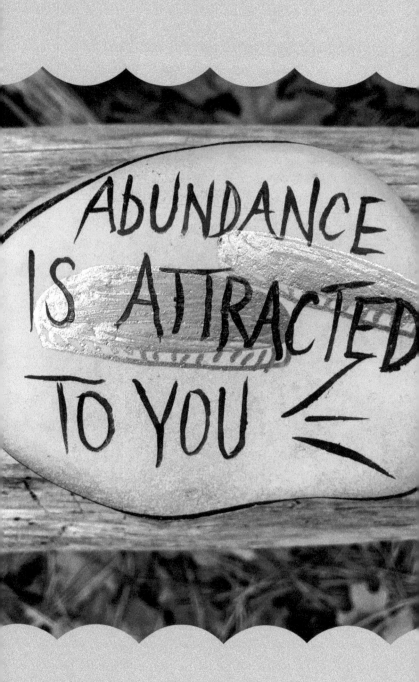

ABUNDANCE IS ATTRACTED TO YOU.

What is it that you wish to attract? Take a moment to write these things down. Then read them aloud and, each night before you go to bed, reflect upon them as if you have already received them.

The light you
See in others
resides within
you too!

THE LIGHT YOU SEE IN OTHERS RESIDES WITHIN YOU TOO!

There are people whom we meet and instantly are drawn to for some reason. There is a quality we admire about them and it attracts us. That quality is one you possess as well. This is a "Namaste" moment, meaning the divine in you honors the divine in them. Journal about one of these encounters you have had with someone.

I don't know
who needs to Hea.
this today But...
it's OK to take a
DAY OFF

> ## "I DON'T KNOW WHO NEEDS TO HEAR THIS TODAY,
> ## BUT...IT'S OK TO TAKE A DAY OFF."
> ### —MEGAN MURPHY

Maybe that is you! Today, give yourself permission to take a day off from something that you feel is your "duty" to complete, such as doing laundry or making the coffee for everyone in the household.

Reflect upon the feelings this action brings up for you. Does guilt arise? Does it make you feel liberated? Did you try but gave in, worrying that if you did not complete it then things would fall apart? Whatever feelings arise, be sure to write with reflective honesty.

"Find things that
shine and move
toward them."

—Mia Farrow

"THE ONLY THING THAT REALLY CHANGES THE WORLD IS WHEN
SOMEONE GETS THE IDEA THAT LOVE CAN ABOUND."
—MR. ROGERS

Journal about three ideas you have that excite you.

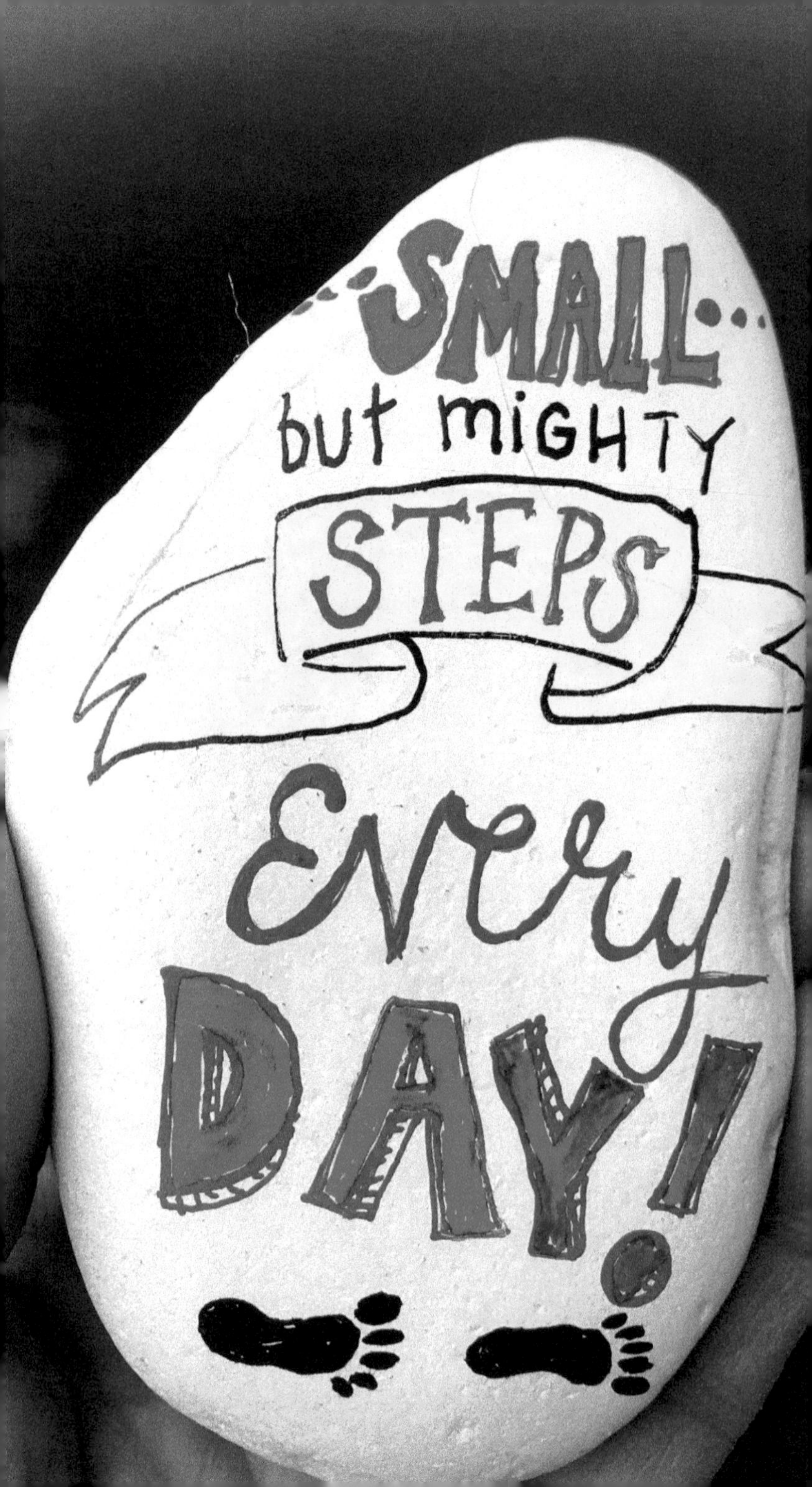
SMALL...
but mighty
STEPS
Every
DAY!

SMALL BUT MIGHTY STEPS EVERY DAY.

Today, create the intention of taking one small step in the direction of a positive change in your life. That's it, one small step.

Create that intention here and journal about the step you have taken.

_____

_____

_____

_____

_____

_____

_____

_____

_____

_____

_____

_____

_____

_____

_____

_____

_____

_____

_____

_____

_____

_____

_____

Every next
level of your
Life will deman[d]
a Different You!

EVERY NEXT LEVEL OF YOUR LIFE WILL DEMAND A DIFFERENT YOU.

Each experience we have helps us grow and evolve. We are not the same person today that we were yesterday. Today will bring new experiences and challenges that will help shape us. Reflect on an experience you had today that changed your perspective.

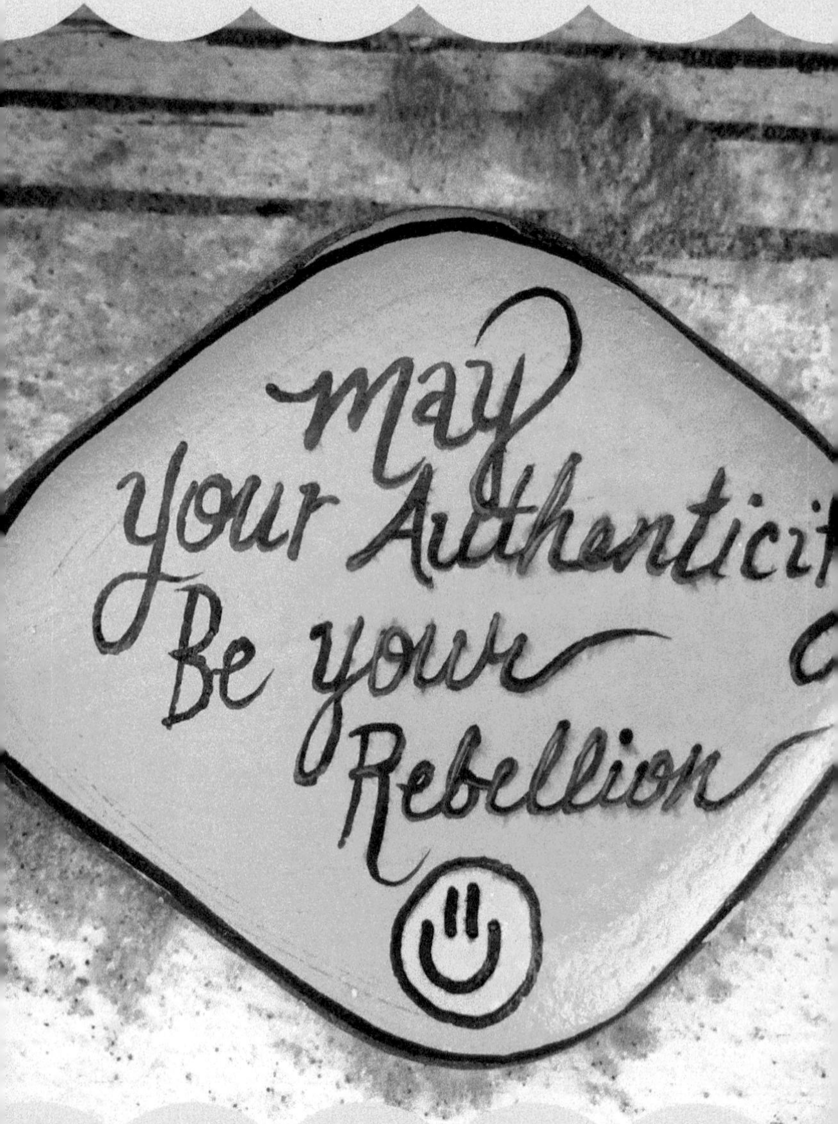
May
your Authenticit
Be your
Rebellion

MAY YOUR AUTHENTICITY BE YOUR REBELLION.

Authentic YOU is dying to be seen and acknowledged. Journal about the things that bring you joy. These are the things that make you, you! No other person will find joy in all of the same things that you do. Sure, we may share some of these things in common, but, just like our DNA, our joy items are individual and they make us different from everyone else.

once in a while
in the middle of an
ordinary day somethi
beautiful & unexpecte
shows up & touches
your heart.

"ONCE IN A WHILE IN THE MIDDLE OF AN ORDINARY DAY, SOMETHING BEAUTIFUL AND UNEXPECTED SHOWS UP AND TOUCHES YOUR HEART."

—MEGAN MURPHY

Journal about one of these moments.

_____

_____

_____

_____

_____

_____

_____

_____

_____

_____

_____

_____

_____

_____

_____

_____

_____

_____

_____

_____

_____

I.LIKE
YOU JUST THE WAY
YOU ARE.
- MR. ROGERS

"I LIKE YOU JUST THE WAY YOU ARE."

—MR. ROGERS

Describe yourself as your best friend would.

Big Things are headed your way!

BIG THINGS ARE HEADED YOUR WAY!

Journal about how this rock message makes you feel.

SURROUND YOURSELF WITH POSITIVE PEOPLE.

Who are the people that you enjoy spending time with? What about spending time with them makes you happy?

_____

_____

_____

_____

_____

_____

_____

_____

_____

_____

_____

_____

_____

_____

_____

_____

_____

_____

_____

_____

_____

_____

be the reason
someone believe
in the goodness
in people.

BE THE REASON SOMEONE BELIEVES IN THE GOODNESS IN PEOPLE.

Being an example for others can leave us with a feeling of accomplishment and purpose. Journal about a few things you can do to encourage another person.

_____

_____

_____

_____

_____

_____

_____

_____

_____

_____

_____

_____

_____

_____

_____

_____

_____

_____

_____

_____

_____

_____

do the right thing. It will gratify some people and astonish the rest.

~Mark Twain

> "ALWAYS DO RIGHT; THIS WILL GRATIFY SOME PEOPLE
> AND ASTONISH THE REST."
>
> —MARK TWAIN

What is one experience you have had that astonished someone?
What is one time that you astonished yourself?

_____

_____

_____

_____

_____

_____

_____

_____

_____

_____

_____

_____

_____

_____

_____

_____

_____

_____

_____

"Service is the rent you pay for your room on Earth."

—Muhammad Ali

OFTEN THINGS HAPPEN BECAUSE THE UNIVERSE IS TRYING TO SIMPLY REDIRECT US!

Life is a series of zigs and zags, and rarely do our experiences go in a straight line from point A to point B. Opportunities and situations present themselves unexpectedly which divert our attention and redirect our path. Reflect on one of these moments, and be sure to include all of the feelings that were attached to this zig and how the zag turned out for you.

AMPLIFY YOUR DREAMS BY SHARING THEM WITH OTHERS!

This journal is the perfect place to begin that process... Write about your dreams and, when you are done, be sure to speak about them freely with those close to you.

_____

_____

_____

_____

_____

_____

_____

_____

_____

_____

_____

_____

_____

_____

_____

_____

_____

_____

_____

_____

_____

_____

IMAGINE A WORLD WHERE EVERYONE FELT LOVED.

Love yourself first. That is how we spread the love that is needed in this world. It is not selfish but rather necessary for you to care for yourself first in order to emit that energy to others.

Journal by using these prompts:
I feel loved when...
If everyone felt loved, the world would...

_____

_____

_____

_____

_____

_____

_____

_____

_____

_____

_____

_____

_____

_____

_____

_____

_____

_____

_____

SUNSETS ARE PROOF THAT ENDINGS CAN BE BEAUTIFUL TOO!

~BeauTap

"SUNSETS ARE PROOF THAT ENDINGS CAN BE BEAUTIFUL TOO."

—BEAU TAPLIN

Finish this sentence: When I witness a sunset, it makes me feel...

_____

_____

_____

_____

_____

_____

_____

_____

_____

_____

_____

_____

_____

_____

_____

_____

_____

_____

_____

_____

_____

_____

EXHALE LOVE!

Take a moment, close your eyes, sit comfortably, and simply breathe. Pay attention to your breath. Feel the cool air as it enters your nose and the warm air as you exhale. Take three long, deep, cleansing breaths.

If thoughts enter your mind while you are focusing on your breath, begin again. Take three more breaths and focus your attention on the sensations. Once you complete this exercise, write about whatever comes up for you. There may be some insight or an idea that arises. Jot that down. Often inner wisdom arises out of the quiet.

TRUST IN THE GUIDANCE YOU RECEIVE.

When was the last time that you listened to your intuition? Reflect upon a time when you felt an urge or had a hunch and you acted upon it. How did you feel after trusting that feeling? What were the results?

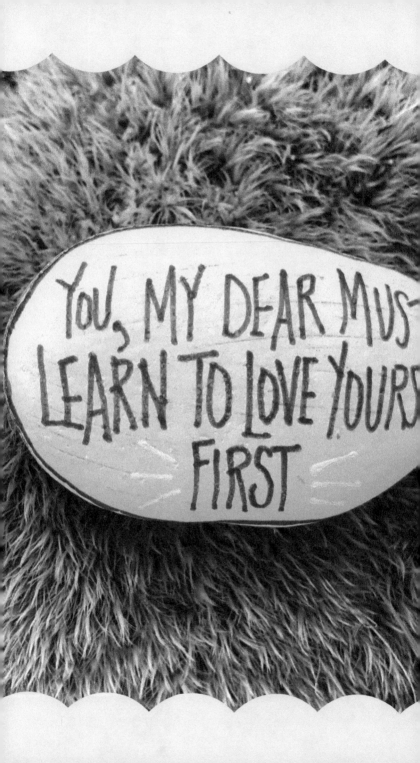

YOU, MY DEAR, MUST LEARN TO LOVE YOURSELF FIRST.

This is a repeated journaling prompt for a reason. Self-love is the starting point for everything. Like in the game Chutes and Ladders, if you try to jump ahead, you will undoubtably find yourself sliding back down a chute to start again. Name three things that you love about yourself.

CELEBRATE THE SMALL, EVERYDAY VICTORIES.

What are some of the small, everyday victories that you have recently experienced?

BE KNOWN FOR YOUR KINDNESS AND GRACE.

Define what kindness means to you.
Describe a moment of grace you have experienced.

"Happiness is not something ready-made. It comes from your own actions."

—Dalai Lama

"IT DOES NOT MATTER HOW SLOWLY YOU GO AS LONG

AS YOU DON'T STOP."

—CONFUCIUS

Write about a time when you persevered.

"OUR GREATEST GLORY IS NOT IN NEVER FALLING, BUT IN RISING

EVERY TIME WE FALL."

—CONFUCIUS

Every time we fall, or experience resistance in our lives, we are building our resilience muscle. Each time, we get stronger and stronger. Journal about one of these experiences and the strength you gained.

I BELIEVE, I TRUST, AND I LET GO!

Repeat this mantra and then reflect upon the thoughts that arise.

_____

_____

_____

_____

_____

_____

_____

_____

_____

_____

_____

_____

_____

_____

_____

_____

_____

_____

_____

_____

_____

_____

_____

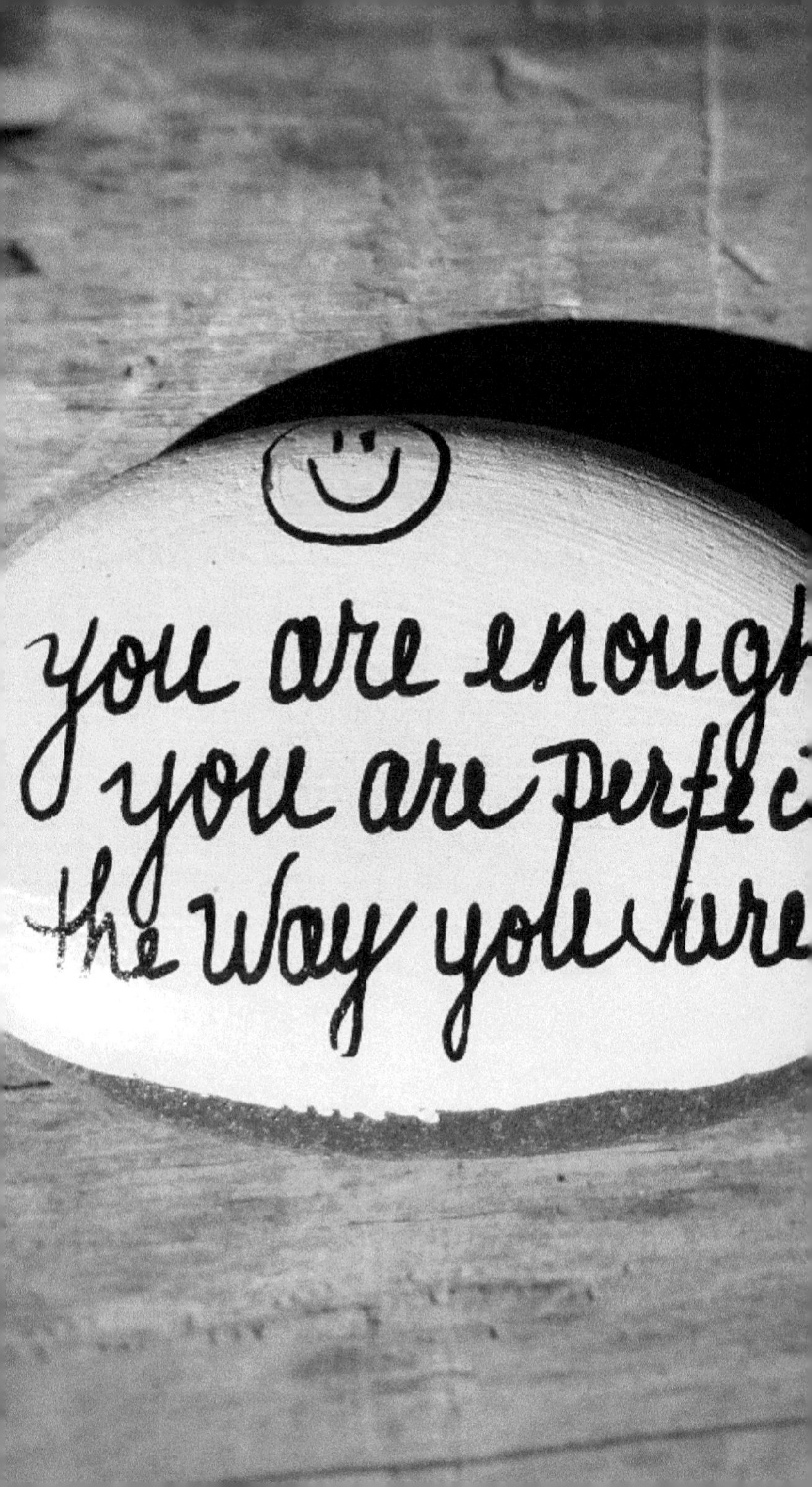
you are enoug
you are perfec
the Way you are

YOU ARE ENOUGH. YOU ARE PERFECT THE WAY YOU ARE.

Perfectly imperfect is what we all are. Embrace your imperfections as they make you unique. What are some of the quirky qualities you have that took you many years to embrace? What would you tell your younger self?

_____

_____

_____

_____

_____

_____

_____

_____

_____

_____

_____

_____

_____

_____

_____

_____

_____

_____

_____

_____

YOU'VE GOT TO HAVE FAITH.

What is the importance of having faith?
What does faith mean to you?

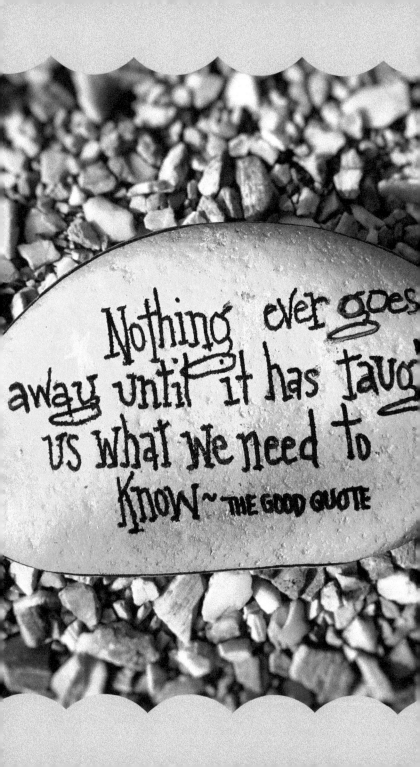

> "NOTHING EVER GOES AWAY UNTIL IT HAS TAUGHT US
> WHAT WE NEED TO KNOW."
> —PEMA CHÖDRÖN

Have you ever noticed the same type of predicaments keep coming up for you? Often this happens because we have not learned the lesson we need from an experience. Difficult moments may keep arising in our lives until we "get it" and truly understand our part in creating that situation. Think about a time in your life when this has occurred. What was the eventual lesson that you learned?

Kindness is the Golden chain by which society is Bound Together.

~Goeth

> ## "KINDNESS IS THE GOLDEN CHAIN BY WHICH SOCIETY IS BOUND TOGETHER."
>
> ### —GOETHE

Kindness connects us to one another. A simple act of kindness by a stranger can help change our perspective. It connects us to the person who offered it and, when we then pay it forward and offer kindness to one another, we then repeat this chain of connection. List several random acts of kindness that you have experienced. How did they make you feel?

"Inch by inch, life's a cinch. yard by yard, Life's hard."

~ John Bytheway

> "INCH BY INCH, LIFE'S A CINCH. YARD BY YARD, LIFE IS HARD."
>
> —JOHN BYTHEWAY

To begin anything, it takes the momentum of taking one small step to get going. What is one small step you can take today toward something you wish to accomplish?

_____

_____

_____

_____

_____

_____

_____

_____

_____

_____

_____

_____

_____

_____

_____

_____

_____

_____

_____

_____

_____

YOU WILL BE TOO MUCH FOR SOME PEOPLE.

THOSE ARE NOT YOUR PEOPLE.

We are attracted to the energy of some people and not others.
We attract our tribe with our vibe!

Write a letter to a friend who is no longer in your life. Maybe it's a
letter of forgiveness, or maybe it is simply a letter reflecting on how
they helped you during a specific time of your life.

Educating the Mind without Educating the Heart is no Education at all.
~Aristotle~

"EDUCATING THE MIND WITHOUT EDUCATING THE HEART IS NO
EDUCATION AT ALL."

—ARISTOTLE

Use your journaling as a personal textbook to focus on educating
your heart.

_____

_____

_____

_____

_____

_____

_____

_____

_____

_____

_____

_____

_____

_____

_____

_____

_____

_____

_____

_____

_____

"With a broken wing she carries her dreams, man you ought to see her fly."

—Martina McBride, "A Broken Wing"

"MAKING ONE PERSON SMILE CAN CHANGE THE WORLD. MAYBE NOT THE WHOLE WORLD, BUT THEIR WORLD."

—JOHN SPENCE

Take this moment to smile. Smile with your whole face: your eyes, your mouth, your cheeks. How does this make you feel?

GREAT THINGS ARE HEADED YOUR WAY!

Does this rock make you curious? Perhaps it evokes a feeling or an emotion. Journal about whatever comes to mind.

EVOLVE!

Your day will go the way the corners of your mouth turn. What makes you truly happy?

_____

_____

_____

_____

_____

_____

_____

_____

_____

_____

_____

_____

_____

_____

_____

_____

_____

_____

_____

_____

_____

_____

_____

_____

"The only Path Wide Enough for all of us is Love."

K. Kojoun

"THE ONLY PATH WIDE ENOUGH FOR ALL OF US IS LOVE."

–K. KOJOURI

Use the each of the letters in the word L O V E and write four words that describe something you love.

"The World is Changed by your Example. Not by your Opinion."

Paulo Coelho

> "THE WORLD IS CHANGED BY YOUR EXAMPLE, NOT BY
> YOUR OPINION."
> —PAULO COELHO

Our actions speak louder than our words. What are three things that you can do today to create change either for yourself or to help another?

_____

_____

_____

_____

_____

_____

_____

_____

_____

_____

_____

_____

_____

_____

_____

_____

_____

_____

HEY, JUST SO YOU KNOW, YOU MATTER!

You matter simply because you are here, in this very moment. Tap into your creativity and draw something on this page. Draw anything you want, a doodle, a word, or whatever comes to mind.

YOU CAN DO ANYTHING YOU PUT YOUR MIND TO.

What is something you have accomplished that surprised you?

"you have always had the power my Dear, you just had to learn it for yourself"

Glinda-Oz

> "YOU HAVE ALWAYS HAD THE POWER, MY DEAR.
> YOU JUST HAD TO LEARN IT FOR YOURSELF."
> —GLINDA THE GOOD WITCH, *THE WIZARD OF OZ*

If you could possess one power, what would that be and why?

Yesterday is history, tomorrow is a mystery, today is a gift, which is why we call it a/the present.

"YESTERDAY IS HISTORY, TOMORROW IS A MYSTERY, TODAY IS A GIFT
WHICH IS WHY IT IS CALLED THE PRESENT."

—BIL KEANE

Journaling brings us into the present moment. When we take the time for this reflection, we become aware of our thoughts. Meaning, we recognize how our past thoughts shape our present reality.

_____

_____

_____

_____

_____

_____

_____

_____

_____

_____

_____

_____

_____

_____

_____

_____

_____

_____

_____

_____

Let the
beauty of what
you love be
what you do
Rumi

"LET THE BEAUTY OF WHAT YOU LOVE BE WHAT YOU DO."

—RUMI

What do you love to do? List ten things you really enjoy doing.

"Oh, the time has come for my dreams to be heard. They will not be pushed aside."

—Beyoncé, "Listen"

LIVE THE WAY YOU WANT TO BE REMEMBERED.

How do you wish to be remembered? What do you hope your legacy will be?

> "LORD MAKE ME AN INSTRUMENT OF THY PEACE. WHERE THERE IS
> HATRED LET ME SOW LOVE."
> —A PRAYER OF ST. FRANCIS OF ASSISI

What is your go-to prayer, mantra, or intention?

YOU LIGHT UP ANY ROOM YOU ENTER.

We are all responsible for the energy that we bring into any conversation, relationship, or room that we enter. Has someone entered a room and drawn you immediately to their energy? Describe that moment.

Maybe it's time to turn your FOMO (fear of missing out) into your JOMO (joy of missing out)

create your own sunshine

MAYBE IT'S TIME TO TURN YOUR FOMO (FEAR OF MISSING OUT) INTO YOUR JOMO (JOY OF MISSING OUT).

No one likes feeling left out or like we are missing out on something. What if we began to look at "missing out" as an opportunity to create a moment for ourselves?

Go out and do something you enjoy doing today and, upon returning home, journal about your experience.

_____

_____

_____

_____

_____

_____

_____

_____

_____

_____

_____

_____

_____

_____

_____

_____

_____

_____

_____

"I'm telling myself I'll be ok. Even on my weakest days, I get a little bit stronger."

—Sara Evans,
"A Little
Bit Stronger"

"You can't stay
in your corner
of the forest
waiting for others
to come to you.
You have to go to
them sometimes."

—Winnie the Pooh
(A.A. Milne)

"Be yourself;
everyone else is
already taken."

—Oscar Wilde

"We judge ourselves by our intentions and others by their actions."

—Steven M.R. Covey

"For every minute you are angry, you lose sixty seconds of happiness."

—Ralph
Waldo Emerson

CREATE SOME KINDNESS ROCKS WITH MESSAGES THAT
YOU WOULD BE GRATEFUL TO RECEIVE.

How to Join the Movement

"ONE MOMENT CAN CHANGE A DAY, ONE DAY CAN CHANGE A LIFE, AND
ONE LIFE CAN CHANGE THE WORLD!"

—BUDDHA

I hope you have enjoyed the inspiration found within these pages.
Here at The Kindness Rocks Project we believe that the perfect rock
always seems to find the perfect person at just the right moment. It is
truly amazing how one simple act of kindness, even represented by a
small painted rock, can make a huge impact on the life of another.

We also hope that you are now compelled to head out into your
community and initiate kind acts in your own expressive way. If this
journal has inspired you, we now call upon you to spread kindness in
your community by painting it forward, because "one message at just
the right moment can change someone's entire day, outlook, or life!"
We hope you will join us.

Supplies Needed:

> Smooth rocks
> Paper towels
> Acrylic paint (any bright color will do)
> Foam paint brush
> Oil-based paint pens
> Clear sealant for topcoat

A complete rock painting kit can be found at www.TheKindnessRocksProject.com. A portion of the proceeds from this kit will go toward bringing The Kindness Rocks Project SEL (Social and Emotional Learning) curriculum to elementary schools across the United States.

How to:

1. Visit your local garden supply center for smooth river rocks. Three to five inch rocks work best. No need to worry about the color of the rock as you will be painting the surface with a cheery base coat.

2. Rinse the rocks in the sink to remove any dirt or salt; next pat dry or allow them to dry on a paper towel.

3. Use a foam brush and your acrylic paint to paint one side of the rock, creating a cheery canvas for your rock artwork. Allow to dry. (You may need multiple coats depending on the color of the rock and the paint you are using.)

4. While you are waiting for your rocks to dry, come up with your rock design or inspiration by thinking about uplifting and positive messages. How might finding your rock with a particular message help someone in need?

5. Next, write your message on the rock using your acrylic paint pens.

6. Be sure to add on the back of your rock #TheKindnessRocksProject so that when people find it, they will post it online. It's fun to search the hashtag and see someone with your rock! This will connect you with many kind, likeminded people who have joined the project.

7. Once the paint pen artwork has dried completely, you can either paint on a clear topcoat or lightly spray in a well-ventilated area.

8. Allow your rock to dry for a few hours. Once dry, you are ready to spread some kindness with others. (Be sure to visit LNT.org for rules and regulations regarding Leave No Trace principles.)

Follow us on Facebook, Instagram, and Twitter and sign up for our email list at www.TheKindnessRocksProject.com for updates on the project and to receive a weekly Inspirational Rock Message created just for you!

About the Founder

Megan Murphy is the founder of The Kindness Rocks Project, a grassroots kindness movement that has swept the nation and beyond. She is a women's empowerment coach, business mentor with SCORE, kindness activist, freelance writer, meditation instructor, and inspirational speaker. She resides on Cape Cod, MA, with her husband, three daughters, and two gigantic dogs.

Megan is a Certified Professional Coach (CPC) and a certified business mentor who earned her coaching certifications through the Institute for Professional Excellence in Coaching (iPEC) and is a member of the International Coaching Federation (ICF).

The Kindness Rocks Project has been featured on Fox News Boston, NBC Boston, WCVB Channel 5's 5 for Good segment, the *Boston Globe*, the *Detroit Free Press*, the *Washington Post*, *Cape Cod Life* magazine, *Conscious Life* magazine, *Parents* magazine, the *Cape Cod Times*, Today.com, *The Huffington Post*, *Southern Living* magazine, *Country Living* magazine, and many other regional news media outlets across the country where members of the project participate. Megan has been published in the 2017 book *Chicken Soup for the Soul: My Kind (of) America*, on Mindbodygreen.com, Tut.com, and Grown & Flown, and quoted in many more publications, podcasts, and blogs. For more information about The Kindness Rocks Project and Megan Murphy, visit www.TheKindnessRocksProject.com and www. MeganMurphyCoaching.com.